D1556212

Applying the Standards:
Evidence-Based Reading
Grade 2

Credits
Content Editor: Erin McCarthy
Copy Editor: Elise Craver

Visit *carsondellosa.com* for correlations to Common Core, state, national, and Canadian provincial standards.

Carson-Dellosa Publishing, LLC
PO Box 35665
Greensboro, NC 27425 USA
carsondellosa.com

ISBN 978-1-4838-1460-5
01-005151151

Table of Contents

Introduction

The purpose of this book is to engage students in close reading while applying the standards. The Common Core reading and language strands are reflected in the interactive questions that follow each passage.

The lessons are intended to help students not only comprehend what they read superficially, but also to help them read complex texts closely and analytically. Students need to get involved deeply with what they are reading and use higher-order thinking skills to reflect on what they have read.

On the following activity pages, students will read a variety of literature and informational passages. These are brief but lend themselves to more complex thinking. Given the opportunity to study shorter texts, students can better practice the higher-level skills they need to closely read more demanding texts.

Each selection is followed by text-dependent questions. Students are prompted to pay attention to how a text is organized, to solve the question of why the author chose specific words, to look for deeper meaning, and to determine what the author is trying to say.

Use the included rubric to guide assessment of student responses and further plan any necessary remediation. The art of close reading is an invaluable skill that will help students succeed in their school years and beyond.

Common Core Alignment Chart

Use this chart to plan your instruction, practice, or remediation of a specific standard. To do this, first choose your targeted standard; then, find the pages listed on the chart that correlate to the standard.

Common Core State Standards*		Practice Pages
Reading Standards for Literature		
Key Ideas and Details	2.RL.1–2.RL.3	5–27
Craft and Structure	2.RL.4–2.RL.6	5–21, 23, 27
Integration of Knowledge and Ideas	2.RL.7, 2.RL.9	5, 6, 8–12, 14–16, 18–25, 27
Range of Reading and Level of Text Complexity	2.RL.10	Each reading passage can be adapted to exercise this standard.
Reading Standards for Informational Text		
Key Ideas and Details	2.RI.1–2.RI.3	28–62
Craft and Structure	2.RI.4–2.RI.6	28, 30–38, 40, 43–49, 51–58, 61, 62
Integration of Knowledge and Ideas	2.RI.7–2.RI.9	28–30, 32–35, 37–39, 41–43, 45, 47–49, 51–55, 57–62
Range of Reading and Level of Text Complexity	2.RI.10	Each reading passage can be adapted to exercise this standard.
Reading Standards: Foundational Skills		
Fluency	2.RF.4	Each reading passage can be adapted to exercise this standard.
Language Standards		
Vocabulary Acquisition and Use	2.L.4–2.L.6	5–8, 10–17, 19, 20, 23, 28, 31, 32, 34–38, 40, 44–47, 49, 53, 55–58, 61

Reading Comprehension Rubric

Use this rubric as a guide to assess students' written work. It can also be offered to students to help them check their work or as a tool to show your scoring.

4	_____ Offers insightful reasoning and strong evidence of critical thinking _____ Makes valid, nontrivial inferences based on evidence in the text _____ Skillfully supports answers with relevant details from the text _____ Gives answers that indicate a complete understanding of the text _____ Gives answers that are easy to understand, clear, and concise _____ Uses conventions, spelling, and grammar correctly
3	_____ Offers sufficient reasoning and evidence of critical thinking _____ Makes inferences based on evidence in the text _____ Supports answers with details from the text _____ Gives answers that indicate a good understanding of the text _____ Gives answers that are easy to understand _____ Uses conventions, spelling, and grammar correctly most of the time
2	_____ Demonstrates some evidence of critical thinking _____ Makes incorrect inferences or does not base inferences on evidence in the text _____ Attempts to support answers with information from the text _____ Gives answers that indicate an incomplete understanding of the text _____ Gives answers that are understandable but lack focus _____ Gives answers containing several errors in conventions, spelling, and grammar
1	_____ Demonstrates limited or no evidence of critical thinking _____ Makes no inferences _____ Does not support answers with details from the text _____ Gives answers that indicate little to no understanding of the text _____ Gives answers that are difficult to understand _____ Gives answers with many errors in conventions, spelling, and grammar

Name _____

Read. Then, answer the questions.

On Our Way to Camp

Crystal waved good-bye to her parents and threw her backpack over her shoulder. She found her best friend, Sarah, on the bus and sat down next to her. "Camp is going to be so much fun," Sarah said, "but I think I will miss my family."

Crystal unzipped her backpack. "Maybe a snack will help you feel better," she said.

The girls giggled and finished their snack in no time. They watched out the window as busy highways became small roads, and buildings became lakes. "This really makes me feel funny," Sarah said as she slumped in her seat.

"I have cards in the pocket of my backpack. Should we play?" Crystal asked.

"OK," answered Sarah. She beat Crystal twice. By the time they had started their third game, Sarah had forgotten all about missing her family.

1. How are Sarah and Crystal traveling to camp?

   _____

2. Sarah says, "This really makes me feel funny." What is she referring to? How do you know?

   _____

   _____

   _____

3. What does Crystal do to help make Sarah forget about missing her family?

   _____

☀ Reflect

Sarah's feelings change from the beginning to the end of the story. Why do you think that is?

_____

_____

_____

_____

Read. Then, answer the questions.

No Broken Friendship

Matthew and Brandon have been best friends since kindergarten. One day when Brandon was playing at Matthew's house, he jumped from the swing set and landed in a strange way. "My arm!" he shouted. One look at Brandon's arm told Matthew that it was broken.

Brandon's parents took him to the hospital where the doctor x-rayed his arm. The doctor put a blue cast on him and told Brandon that his bones would grow back in place. He also reminded Brandon not to take any risks, such as falling or playing too roughly, during the next eight weeks.

The next day, Brandon took his X-ray to school and told the class his story. They had many questions, and Brandon answered them as best he could. Matthew asked, "Do you want to play tic-tac-toe instead of wall ball at recess today?"

"Great idea!" Brandon answered.

1. Where does Brandon go to find out if his arm is broken?

_____

2. How does the doctor know that Brandon's arm is broken?

_____

_____

3. The doctor tells Brandon not to take any risks. What is a *risk*? Use details from the story to explain your answer.

_____

_____

Reflect

Matthew asks Brandon to play tic-tac-toe instead of wall ball at recess. Why? Use details from the story to explain your answer.

_____

_____

_____

_____

Name _____

Read. Then, answer the questions.

The Rain

Pitter-patter, pitter-pat. . .
How I love the rain!

Storm clouds moving in,
The rain is about to begin.
How I love to see the rain!

Tiny sprinkles on my face,
Little droplets playing chase.
How I love to feel the rain!

I open up my mouth so wide,
Letting little drops inside.
How I love to taste the rain!

Tapping on my window,
It is a rhythm that I know.
How I love to hear the rain!

Everything looks so green,
And the fresh air smells so
clean.
How I love to smell the rain!

Pitter patter, pitter pat. . .
How I love the rain!

1. What is the cause of the rain in the poem?

_____

2. How does the author describe the sound of the rain?

_____

3. Where does the author use rhyming words in the poem?

_____

_____

☀ Reflect

The author uses a certain type of adjective throughout the poem to describe the rain. What is it? Use details from the poem to explain your answer.

_____

_____

_____

_____

Read. Then, answer the questions.

A Radical Summer

June 5, 2014

Dear Grandma and Grandpa,

What's happening? I'm just hanging out. Today is the first day of my summer vacation. I have some radical things planned this summer. Later on today, my friend Michael is coming over. We're going to ride our bikes. Tomorrow, I start swimming lessons. Mom said that in two weeks we are going to visit you. I can't wait! Can we please go to the park with the waterslides? I had a blast last year when we went there. Also, I would like to go fishing. This year, I'm going to catch the biggest fish. You'll have to buy a new pan to cook it in because I don't think the pans you have are big enough. Well, I have to split. Catch you later.

Love, Nick

1. What is one of the radical things Nick has planned for the summer?

_____

2. How does Nick feel about the waterslides at the park? What phrase describes this?

_____

_____

3. Why will Grandma and Grandpa have to buy a new pan?

_____

_____

4. At the end of the letter Nick writes, "I have to split." What does he mean?

_____

_____

☀ Reflect

How does Nick feel about being on summer vacation? Use details from the story to explain your answer.

_____

_____

_____

_____

Read. Then, answer the questions.

The Ants and the Cookies

One day, two ants went exploring. They came across two giant cookies.

"One of these cookies would feed my whole family for a month," said the second little ant. "But, how can such little ants like us carry such big cookies like these?"

"It seems impossible!" said the first little ant. "But, I must try."

So, the first little ant started to tug and pull at one cookie. Suddenly, a tiny piece broke off the cookie. She took the piece back to her family.

"I'm not going to waste my time on such a small piece of cookie. I will find a way to take the whole cookie back to my family," said the second little ant.

Soon, the first little ant returned. She found the second little ant still pushing the other cookie, unable to move it. Again, the first little ant took a small piece of cookie back to her family. This went on for most of the day. The first little ant kept moving small pieces of cookie until she had moved the entire cookie. The second little ant finally became tired of trying to complete a task that seemed too big. She went home with nothing.

1. When do the two ants find the two cookies?

   _____

2. What problem do the two ants have?

   _____

   _____

3. How do the two ants disagree on getting the cookies back to their families?

   _____

   _____

☀ Reflect

What lesson does the second ant learn from the first ant about how she moved the cookie?

_____

_____

_____

_____

_____

Read. Then, answer the questions.

The Mouse and His Food

One day, a little mouse sat inside his little house inside a log. "Oh dear," said the mouse. "I have nothing to eat but this small seed. Surely, I will **starve**." So, the little mouse went out to find some food.

Soon, the little mouse found two acorns. He took the acorns to his house. "Oh, dear," said the mouse. "I have nothing to eat but a small seed and these two acorns. What if rain comes and washes them away? Surely, I will starve." So, the little mouse went out to find more food.

Soon, he found a corncob and a piece of cheese. He took them to his house. "Oh, dear," said the mouse. "I have nothing to eat but a small seed, these two acorns, this corncob, and a piece of cheese. What if wind comes and blows them away? Surely, I will starve." So, the little mouse went out to find more food.

Soon, he found six walnuts. He took the walnuts to his house. "Oh, dear," said the mouse. "I have nothing to eat but a small seed, these two acorns, this corncob, a piece of cheese, and these six walnuts. What if snow comes and freezes them all? Surely, I will starve." So, the little mouse went out to find more food.

This went on for days. Finally, the mouse had gathered more food than 10 mice could eat in a year. Soon, rain, wind, and snow did come. But, none of the food washed away. None of the food blew away. And, none of the food froze. But, because the mouse could not eat all of the food, the food rotted.

1. Based on the story, what does *starve* mean?

_____

2. How does the mouse react to having only one small seed for food?

_____

_____

3. What is the mouse always worried about?

_____

_____

Reflect

What lesson does the reader learn at the end of the story? Use details from the story to explain your answer.

_____

_____

_____

Name _____

Read. Then, answer the questions.

The Frugal King

In a kingdom far away lived a **frugal** king. Each week, the king placed some of his kingdom's food into a large storehouse in the castle. The people of the kingdom were not happy.

"Why does the king take our food and store it away?" asked one of the townspeople.

"I bet that he is taking our food and eating it himself," accused another.

"We are starving," sighed another. "We barely have enough to eat."

"All of the people in the kingdom on the other side of the land eat until their stomachs almost burst," shouted another. "Our king is cruel to his people."

Despite what the townspeople said, the king kept taking a portion of the food and storing it away.

One day, a famine came to the land. It was impossible to grow wheat to make bread. It was impossible to feed the cows, so there was no milk or cheese, and the famine grew worse. The townspeople in kingdoms throughout the land were hungry. But, the people from the frugal king's kingdom had plenty to eat. The king opened the doors of the storehouse and fed his people. The townspeople knew that the king's frugality had saved their lives.

1. Why are the people of the kingdom not happy at the beginning of the story?

    _____

2. Based on the passage, what does *frugal* mean?

    _____

3. How do the townspeople's feelings change from the beginning to the end of the story? Use details from the story to explain your answer.

    _____

    _____

☀ Reflect

Would the story have ended differently if the king had not been frugal? Explain.

_____

_____

Name _____

Read. Then, answer the questions.

Two

Two living things, blowing in the wind.
One stands straight, the other bends.

One is a strong tree, growing tall.
The other is grass, ever so small.

Both are Mother Nature's gift.
The tree, you can climb. On the grass, you can sit.

Green is their color, brought on by the spring.
Grass or trees, they both make me sing!

1. In the first stanza, what living thing "stands straight"?

_____

2. What is one feature the tree and grass have in common?

_____

3. How do the tree and grass make the author feel? How do you know?

_____

_____

☀ Reflect

If it were a different season, how would you change the poem? Explain the changes.

_____

_____

_____

_____

_____

_____

_____

_____

_____

Name _____

Read. Then, answer the questions.

The Fire Station

Today, our class took a field trip to the fire station. First, we met Captain Jeff. He showed us the big fire trucks. The fire trucks, or fire engines, have many switches and valves. The fire trucks have many compartments that hold the equipment and tools used to fight fires and help in emergencies.

We saw the large hoses the firefighters use to **extinguish**, or put out, fires. We saw the tall ladders the firefighters climb to reach high places. We saw the uniforms the firefighters wear when they fight fires. We got to try on their coats, pants, boots, and hats. The clothes firefighters wear are big and heavy. Gavin fell over because of the weight of the clothes!

Then, Captain Jeff showed us where the firefighters live when they are on duty. Inside the fire station, are beds, showers, and a kitchen. The firefighters take turns cooking meals and shopping for food.

Suddenly, we heard a loud siren. The siren meant that there was an emergency. Captain Jeff and the other firefighters quickly put on their uniforms, jumped on the fire trucks and drove away. It was interesting to see the fire station and learn about the job of a firefighter.

1. What equipment do the firefighters used to reach high places?

   _____

2. Describe the main topic of the second paragraph.

   _____

   _____

3. Based on the passage, what does *extinguish* mean?

   _____

☀ Reflect

How does the author feel about the field trip to the fire station? How do you know?

_____

_____

_____

_____

Name _____

Read. Then, answer the questions.

Ma Lien's Dream

There once lived a poor Chinese boy named Ma Lien. He worked hard in the rice fields, dreaming of the one day he would become a painter. But, Ma Lien did not even have a paintbrush. Instead, he used rocks to scratch on stones or his fingers to draw pictures in wet sand.

One night as Ma Lien lay in bed, he dreamed that he had a special paintbrush. Whatever he painted with it came to life!

Ma Lien used his special paintbrush to help people. He painted roosters for poor families in his village and toys for children.

A greedy king heard about the special paintbrush. He ordered Ma Lien to paint a mountain of gold for him. Ma Lien painted a gold mountain surrounded by a huge sea. The king ordered him to paint a ship so that he could sail to the mountain. As the king and his men stepped on the ship, Ma Lien painted a storm that sunk the king's ship.

Ma Lien awoke and went to the rice fields to work. Eventually, he did **acquire** a paintbrush. Although it was not a "special" paintbrush, what he painted with it was special. He remembered the dream and always used his talent wisely.

1. Why did Ma Lien use rocks to scratch on stones or his fingers to draw in wet sand?

_____

2. Based on the story, what does *acquire* mean?

_____

3. What did you learn about Ma Lien's character from his dream about the special paintbrush?

_____

_____

4. How does Ma Lien respond to the king's orders to paint him a gold mountain and a ship?

_____

_____

☀ Reflect

What does Ma Lien learn from his dream? How does this influence what lesson the reader learns from the story?

_____

_____

     © Carson-Dellosa · CD-104831 · Applying the Standards: Evidence-Based Reading

Name _____

Read. Then, answer the questions.

A Day with an Orangutan

Fireball woke early in the rain forest. He reached out to pull on a leaf, waking his mother. "Come on, Mom," Fireball called out. He grabbed a vine and swung across the trees, searching for ripe fruit. Suddenly, it began to rain. Fireball did not want to get wet, so he held a piece of wood over his head. "Much better," he thought.

When the rain stopped, Fireball spotted some orange fur through the trees. It was his mom. She was holding a vine between her feet and had stretched across to the other vine, which she was holding in her hands. Fireball saw his chance. He jumped onto her belly and began rocking back and forth. "Whee!" he yelled. Then, he noticed something in his mother's hand. He pulled her fingers away from her thumb. Inside, he found a small piece of fruit.

"You are so curious, Fireball," his mother said. "Let's find something for you to eat." They spent the afternoon searching for more ripe fruit.

Soon, it was getting dark, which told Fireball and his mother that it was time to build the evening's nest. They gathered branches and leaves, making a nest high in the trees. Fireball cuddled next to his mother and fell asleep.

1. How does Fireball protect himself from the rain?

_____

2. Do Fireball and his mother know that it is going to rain? How do
you know?

_____

_____

3. Why does Fireball's mother say, "You are so curious, Fireball"?

_____

✸ Reflect

Describe how Fireball feels about his mom. Use details from the story to explain your answer.

_____

_____

_____

_____

_____

Name _____

Read. Then, answer the questions.

Teddy Bear

I am too old for my teddy bear,
And poor Ted is showing too much wear.

Now that I am a bigger kid,
It is time that I kept Ted hid.

So, I said "good-bye" to my old friend,
Because teddy bears are just pretend.

But that first night, I could not sleep
Though I tried and tried to count sheep.

I thought about my teddy bear,
Hidden in the closet there.

And now, I miss old Ted so,
I just cannot let my old friend go.

So, I tiptoed quietly out of bed
And found my little bear called Ted,

And, I brought him back to bed with me.
Poor Ted still needs me, can you see?

1. Why does the author need to hide Ted?

_____

2. What does the author mean when he says, "poor Ted is showing too much wear"?

_____

_____

3. Where does the author use rhyming words in the poem?

_____

_____

⬥ Reflect

How do the author's feelings about his teddy bear change from the beginning to the end of the poem? Use details from the poem to explain your answer.

_____

_____

_____

_____

 © Carson-Dellosa · CD-104831 · Applying the Standards: Evidence-Based Reading

Read. Then, answer the questions.

Three Wishes

A long time ago, there lived an old woman and an old man. One day, they went fishing. Suddenly, the man felt a tug on his line. What a big fish he had caught! Surely, this fish would provide enough food for him and his wife for an entire week. But, as he began to unhook the fish, the fish spoke!

"Please, let me go," said the fish. "If you do, I will grant you three wishes."

"A talking fish!" shouted the old man. "How can this be?" And, without thinking, he threw the fish back into the water.

The old woman shouted, "You foolish man! You threw the fish back without making any wishes. And, it could have been food for a week. Just once, I wish you would think!"

Just as the words came out of the woman's mouth, a thought popped into the man's mind. "Well," said the man, "your wish has come true. I am thinking. I am thinking that you are a rude woman, and I wish you would keep quiet!"

Just as the man wished, the woman's mouth was shut tightly. "What have we done?" the man said. "With three wishes, we could have wished for money, food, or fame, but instead we wished away our wishes. Now, the only **sensible** wish would be that my wife's mouth would be opened."

And, as quickly as the man said the last wish, the woman's mouth was opened. "We don't have more money, food, or fame, but we do have each other," said the old man. Together, they walked back to their cottage.

1. How does the old woman feel when the old man throws the big fish back into the water? How do you know?

_____

_____

2. Based on the story, what does *sensible* mean?

_____

_____

Reflect

What lesson do the old man and old woman learn? Use details from the story to explain your answer.

_____

_____

_____

Name _____

Read. Then, answer the questions.

What Is Big?

Hannah Hippo wanted to be big. But, Hannah was the smallest hippo in the river. One day, Hannah looked at her reflection in the river. "Look at my teeth. My teeth are big! So, I must be big."

Soon, a bird came to the river. "I am big, and I have big teeth," said Hannah. "Yes, you are big," said the bird as it flew away.

Next, a turtle came to the river. "I am big, and I have big teeth," said Hannah. "Yes, you are big," said the turtle as he crawled away.

Before long, a baby tiger came to the river. "I am big, and I have big teeth," said Hannah. "Yes, you are big," said the baby tiger as he scampered away.

Hannah sat by the river for a long time. "I am big, and I have big teeth. But this is no fun. I have no one to play with." Soon, Hannah's mom and dad came to the river. Hannah looked at her mom and dad. Hannah looked at their big teeth. Hannah felt small. But Hannah did not mind. At least she had someone to play with. Maybe being small was not so bad after all.

1. How does Hannah Hippo discover that she has big teeth?

_____

2. How do all of the animals respond when Hannah tells them that she is big and has big teeth?

_____

_____

3. How does Hannah feel when she compares her size and teeth to her parents' size and teeth?

_____

_____

Reflect

Describe how being small is a good thing for Hannah. Use details from the story to explain your answer.

_____

_____

_____

_____

Name _____

Read. Then, answer the questions.

Tulips

In my flower garden, tulips always grow,
Straight like soldiers all in a row.

With colors so bright, reds, oranges,
    yellows too,
They are one of nature's special gifts just
    for you.

A tulip's colorful petals are shaped like a
    cup,
Holding little raindrops for birds to drink
    up.

Winds cause them to sway
Back and forth every day.

But, still my tulips grow
Like soldiers in a row.

Come to the Meadow

Come to the meadow where the primrose
    grows,
And daisies and cowslips are lined up in
    rows.

Buttercups look as yellow as gold.
Truly, it is a sight to behold.

Busy bees humming about them are seen.
Grasshoppers chirp in the tall grasses so
    green.

Butterflies happily flutter along.
The bluebirds are singing a lively new
    song.

So, come to the meadow, and there you
    will see
Spring come alive for you and for me.

1. In the poem "Come to the Meadow," what does the author compare buttercups to?

_____

2. In the poem "Tulips," what does the author compare tulips to?

_____

3. Compare the rhyming patterns in both poems. How are they alike?

_____

_____

☀ Reflect

Think about the setting in each poem. Could the settings be the same if the author rewrote the poems? Use details from the poems to explain your answer.

_____

_____

_____

_____

Name _____

Read. Then, answer the questions.

Paul Bunyan: A Tall Tale

When Paul Bunyan was a baby, he was too big to fit in the house! As he got older, he was so big that his parents had to teach him not to step on houses or farm animals. Back then, people needed a lot of trees to build their houses and the railroads. The men who cut down the trees were called **loggers**. Because Paul was so big, he could swing his ax a few times to cut down a whole forest. He became a great logger.

One winter, Paul found a gigantic baby blue ox and named him Babe. Babe would carry the wood that Paul cut down. He would also take water to the loggers. Paul strapped a huge tub on Babe's back and filled it with water. Sometimes, some water would spill and land in one of Babe's huge footprints. That is why so many lakes are in Minnesota. Once, Babe tripped and the whole bucket of water spilled. He made the Mississippi River!

After Paul and Babe finished logging in one area, they would move on. One time, Paul started dragging his ax behind him. The ditch it made was so huge that we now call it the Grand Canyon!

No one knows where Paul and Babe are today. No matter where they are, you can be sure they are leaving their mark!

1. Based on the story, what is a *logger*?

_____

2. How are Babe and Paul similar? Underline the details from the story that support your answer.

_____

_____

3. How does Babe help Paul? Give an example from the story.

_____

_____

☀ Reflect

A tall tale is a story that uses unbelievable reasons as explanations for real things. Describe the elements of this story that make it a tall tale.

_____

_____

_____

_____

Read. Then, answer the questions.

A Real King

Leo the Lion had been king of the grasslands for a very long time, but the animals felt they needed a new king. Leo had become lazy, mean, and selfish. When Leo learned of this, he set the animals free and laughed to himself, "They will beg to have me back!" But the animals did not beg to have Leo back, so he moved away.

One lonely day, Leo found a mouse that was balancing on a branch in the river. He helped the mouse to the shore. Later, Leo found a baby zebra who was lost from his mother. Leo was kind and helped the little zebra find his home.

When the animals learned of Leo's kind acts, they asked him to become their king again. They needed a helpful and strong king, which Leo now seemed to be. Leo the Lion had become a real king!

1. Where does the story take place? Underline the details in the story that support your answer.

_____

2. How does Leo help the baby zebra?

_____

_____

3. Why does Leo set the animals free when he learns they want a new king?

_____

_____

_____

☀ Reflect

How does Leo change from the beginning to the end of the story? Use details from the story to explain your answer.

_____

_____

_____

_____

Name _____

Read. Then, answer the questions.

The Gigantic Cookie

My mother baked a gigantic cookie for me. I sat on my porch to eat it. But, before I could take a bite, my friend Anna came by.

"Will you share your cookie with me?" Anna asked. I broke my cookie into two pieces, one for me and one for Anna. But, before we could take a bite, Jessi and Lucy came by.

"Will you share your cookie with us?" they asked. Anna and I each broke our cookie piece into two pieces. Now, we had four pieces: one for me, one for Anna, one for Jessi, and one for Lucy. But, before we could take a bite, four more friends came by.

"Will you share your cookie with us?" they asked. Anna, Jessi, Lucy, and I all broke our pieces in half. Now, we had enough to share between eight friends. But, before we could take a bite, eight more friends came by.

"Will you share your cookie with us?" they asked. We all broke our pieces in half to share with our eight new friends. I looked at my gigantic cookie. It was no longer gigantic.

"Hey, does anyone know what is gigantic when there is one but is small when there are sixteen?" I asked.

"No, what?" my friends asked.

"My cookie," I laughed.

1. What words does the author use to describe the cookie?

   _____

2. What happens to the author's cookie throughout the story?

   _____

3. At the end of the story, how does the author respond to all of her friends asking her to share her cookie?

   _____

☀ Reflect

Based on the events in the story, how would you describe the author's character? Use details from the story to explain your answer.

_____

_____

_____

_____

Read. Then, answer the questions.

Brianna's Favorite Place

Brianna lives in Newfoundland, Canada. Today, she is visiting her favorite place: a high cliff that overlooks the ocean. She likes to watch the fishing boats bob like corks in the blue water. She listens to the cries of the seagulls as they look for food. She admires the beauty of the tall lighthouse. She laughs as she watches the whales play. Brianna lies on her back. She sees animals in the clouds. Brianna loves to feel the mist from the ocean against her face. It is a peaceful day.

Suddenly, a huge wave crashes onto the shore. The fishing boats start coming to port as fast as they can. The clouds darken. A strong wind begins to blow. A foghorn cries out. It warns the sailors that a storm is coming. The waves get bigger and bigger.

As the storm comes in, Brianna is glad that she is high above the angry ocean. She takes one last look at the beautiful white-capped waves. Then, she runs home.

1. How does the author describe Brianna's favorite place? Give examples from the story.

_____

_____

2. How does the day change? Use details from the story to explain your answer.

_____

_____

3. List three words that tell the reader how Brianna feels throughout the story.

_____

☀ Reflect

The author tells the reader that Brianna is glad to be high above the ocean. Are there other details that tell the reader she might be feeling something else? What are they?

_____

_____

_____

_____

Name _____

Read. Then, answer the questions.

The Clay Necklace

Miss Jacob's class spent all afternoon working on projects for Saturday's American Indian fair. Lynn and Jeffrey were to make a clay necklace. "I will work on the beads, and you can make the clay sun that will hang in the middle," Lynn told Jeffrey. Lynn carefully shaped beads out of clay and strung them on a piece of yarn.

Jeffrey quickly made a ball of clay and smashed it flat. "I am done," he called and ran outside for recess.

The next day, Lynn was sick and could not come to the fair. Jeffrey's family looked for the necklace he had told them about. There it was. Jeffrey noticed something was different. The clay sun that hung from the middle of the necklace had been carefully carved and painted. It was beautiful!

"There you are, Jeffrey," said Miss Jacob. "I wanted to tell you how great your work is on the clay sun! You must have spent a lot of time on it."

1. Why did Lynn and Jeffrey make a clay necklace?

   _____

2. How does the way Jeffrey made the clay sun tell the reader how he feels about the project? Use details from the story to explain your answer.

   _____

   _____

3. How does the way Lynn make the beads tell the reader how she feels about the project? Use details from the story to explain your answer.

   _____

   _____

Reflect

What actually happened with the clay sun in the story? What should Jeffrey tell Miss Jacob's based on what he did in the beginning of the story?

_____

_____

_____

_____

_____

Name _____

Read. Then, answer the questions.

The Day Emily Sneezed

One very hot day, Emily the Elephant said, "I think I may sneeze."
   So, the grassland animals said, "Excuse us, if you please."

And ran, oh they did, for they were afraid
   Of what may happen when Emily's sneeze was made.

The giraffes ran for cover and hid behind leaves
   Of the thickest and tallest of all the African trees.

The warthogs got up from feeding on their knees
   And frightfully asked, "Did Emily say she may sneeze?"

The falcon flew quickly as falcons can do.
   He remembered the last time Emily said, "Achoo!"

The earth had rumbled, and all of the trees shook
   Worse than any disaster you've read about in a book.

So, the animals all covered their ears and closed their eyes,
   But then they got such a pleasant surprise. . .

Emily the Elephant did not let out a sneeze,
   But instead she laughed and made a cool breeze.

Now, all of the animals went back to their eating,
   And they were happy their land did not take a beating.

1. What is the setting of the poem? Underline two details that describe it.

   _____

2. What details in the poem tell the reader the giraffes were afraid of Emily's sneeze?

   _____

   _____

3. Do you think the grassland animals would be as afraid if it were the falcon that had to sneeze? Use details from the story to explain your answer.

   _____

   _____

⚡ Reflect

Based on the passage, how did the animals' thinking change from the beginning to the end of the poem? Use details from the story to explain your answer.

_____

Name _____

Read. Then, answer the questions.

Things Could Always Be Worse

Once upon a time, lived a poor farmer. He shared a small house with his wife and six children. Their house was always quite noisy because the children chased each other and argued. The farmer could take it no more and went to see the wise one for help.

"You must bring your dog inside your house to live with you," said the wise one.

So, the farmer did as he was told, but the noise only got worse. Now, the dog barked, and the children argued. The farmer went back to the wise one for the second time.

"You must bring your cow inside to live with you," said the wise one.

Again, the farmer did as the wise one said, but now the cow mooed, the dog barked, and the children argued. It was worse than ever.

The farmer continued to visit the wise one until he had his chickens, sheep, and horse living inside his house too.

At last, the wise one told the farmer to put all of the animals back outside. When the farmer came into his house and heard only the sound of his children arguing, he thought he was very lucky to live in such a quiet house.

1. Why does the farmer go to see the wise one?

_____

2. Describe three things that the wise one tells the farmer to do.

_____

_____

3. Why does the farmer feel lucky at the end of the story?

_____

☀ Reflect

What does the farmer learn at the end of the story? Use details from the story to explain your answer.

_____

_____

_____

_____

_____

Name _____

Read. Then, answer the questions.

A Husband for Daughter Rat

Mother and Father Rat were very proud of their daughter, and they wanted her to marry someone very special.

Father Rat chose a fine and noble rat as Daughter Rat's husband, but Mother Rat disagreed. She thought her daughter should marry the sun.

The rats went to visit the sun. The sun told the rats that perhaps the cloud would make a better husband for Daughter Rat. The cloud could block out the sun.

Then, the three rats went to visit the cloud. The cloud recommended that Daughter Rat marry the powerful wind. It was true, the wind did throw the cloud about.

Now the Rat Family tried to catch the wind to talk. The wind showed them that the wall was stronger because he could block the wind. He thought Daughter Rat should marry the wall.

Mother Rat asked the wall if he would like to marry Daughter Rat, but he answered that there was someone else Daughter Rat should marry instead. The wall said, "Do you see these small holes in me? I cannot stop something from passing through them." The noble rat had made the holes in the wall. The rats watched as the noble rat crawled through a hole.

Father Rat was pleased because this was the noble rat that he had chosen before. The two married, and they lived happily ever after.

1. How does Mother Rat feel about Daughter Rat marrying the noble rat? How do you know?

   _____

   _____

2. Why does the cloud recommend that Daughter Rat marry the wind?

   _____

3. Explain how the story ends. Use details from the story to explain your answer.

   _____

   _____

☀ Reflect

Describe how you know this story is fiction. Use details from the story to explain your answer.

_____

_____

Read. Then, answer the questions.

Biggest Bill on the Block

Toucans are hard birds to miss! They have huge yellow-orange-and-black bills. Some toucans have green and red in their bills too. With a bill that big, might toucans tip over? They do not tip over because their bills are light. They are hollow and feel like dry sponges. The bills have "teeth" built into the edges. The teeth let the toucans eat many different foods. Toucans enjoy fruit, tree frogs, and other birds' eggs.

Toucans are strange in other ways too. They have strange feet with four toes. Two toes face forward. Two toes face backward. This helps the bird grip wet branches in the rain forest. Another strange thing about toucans are their "feather" tongues. The birds have bristles on the end of their tongues. These are sharp little hairs. They help the birds make their loud, croaking calls. In the rain forest, you can hear toucans that are far away!

Toucans are friendly birds. They live in flocks of six or more birds. They look for homes in hollow trees. Then, they all sleep together in one big nest inside the tree. Both parents sit on the eggs. Both parents feed the chicks.

You do not have to visit a rain forest to see a toucan. The toucan's friendly nature makes it easy to tame. It is no wonder that so many toucans live in zoos!

1. What is the main topic of the third paragraph?

_____

2. The author describes two strange things about toucans. What makes each thing strange?

_____

_____

_____

3. Why has the author put the word *feather* in quotation marks?

_____

☀ Reflect

Explain why the author ends the passage with the sentence, "It is no wonder that so many toucans live in zoos!" Use details from the passage to explain your answer.

_____

_____

_____

_____

Read. Then, answer the questions.

Quiet, I Am Sleeping

We sleep about eight hours each night. Three-toed sloths sleep 15 to 20 hours a day. Sloths live in trees. They are more awake at night. That is when they eat leaves. Sometimes, sloths move slowly to other trees. Then, they eat more leaves. Sometimes, while they eat, the sloths nod off again! Sleeping and moving slowly save their energy.

Sloths live in rain forests. They sleep and eat high up in the trees. This keeps them safe. Most enemies cannot reach sloths. But, large snakes will sometimes attack them. Big birds may too.

Sometimes, sloths climb down. They have long, sharp claws. They can fight with these claws. But, they move very slowly. Sloths are easy to catch. There is more danger on the ground. So, sloths only climb down about once a week. Sloths live in Central and South America. They do not seem afraid of people and often live near villages.

When sloths are not climbing, they are hanging upside down. They grip tree branches by their feet. Sloths spend most of their lives this way. This is how they sleep and eat. Maybe this is why their organs, including their stomachs, are in different places than in other animals. This is just one more difference in these slow, sleepy animals.

1. Why do sloths move slowly and sleep so much?

_____

2. How does living near villages make sloths different than many other wild animals? Use details from the passage to explain your answer.

_____

_____

3. Describe the connection between where sloths live and what they eat.

_____

_____

_____

⚙ Reflect

How does the author support how sloths are different from other animals? Use details from the passage to explain your answer.

_____

_____

_____

Read. Then, answer the questions.

Talk to Me

We are mammals. Bottlenose dolphins are mammals, too. We breathe air. Dolphins do too. We live in groups. Dolphins do too. Our groups are called families. Dolphins' familes are called pods. We use language. We can talk. Can dolphins talk too?

Do dolphins have their own language? Scientists do not know. If dolphins did, they would have "words" for things. They would be able to tell each other whole thoughts. Dolphins make sounds. We can hear these sounds. Scientists have counted more than 1,700 different dolphin sounds made within one group of dolphins. A dolphin makes sounds using a blowhole. A blowhole is a hole on top of the dolphin's head.

Scientists think each dolphin has a signature whistle. A dolphin may tell other dolphins something such as this: "I am me, from this pod. Right now, I am happy (or sad or scared)."

Bottlenose dolphins "talk" in other ways too. They do not just use sound. They use their bodies. They kick with their tails. They roll their eyes. They brush against other dolphins. Sometimes, two dolphins swim side by side. Then, they touch fins. It seems as if they are holding hands.

Scientists hope to learn more about dolphins so that they can answer the question, "Can dolphins talk?"

1. What detail from the passage tells that dolphins are mammals?

_____

2. What is the main topic of the fourth paragraph?

_____

_____

3. What do scientists currently know about how dolphins communicate? Use details from the passage to explain your answer.

_____

_____

☀ Reflect

Compare how human and dolphin communications are the same and how they are different. Use details from the passage to explain your answer.

_____

_____

_____

_____

Read. Then, answer the questions.

Honest Abe's Return

Do ghosts frighten you? Try sleeping at the White House. You may end up terrified! This famous American house seems to be haunted. Who is the White House's most famous ghost? It is President Abraham Lincoln!

White House workers say they have seen Lincoln's ghost many times. One man said he saw Lincoln sitting outside of a room that had been his office. Lincoln's office has been converted into a bedroom. It is called the "Lincoln Bedroom." This is where the ghost is seen the most.

Queen Wilhelmina of the Netherlands once stayed in the White House. She heard a **mysterious** knock at the door. Lincoln's ghost was there! She fainted.

Winston Churchill was a famous British leader. He also said he saw the ghost. Churchill was visiting the White House. He walked into the Lincoln Bedroom to find Lincoln standing inside!

One first lady, Grace Coolidge, said that she saw Lincoln there too. He was looking out the window. Mrs. Coolidge thought he looked sad.

Many people say that they have seen President Lincoln . . . more than 100 years after his death.

1. Where do people claim to see Lincoln's ghost the most?

_____

2. Based on the passage, what does *mysterious* mean?

_____

3. How are the three people who claimed to see Lincoln's ghost alike?

_____

☀ Reflect

How does the author support the claims about Lincoln's ghost to the reader? How is the passage structured?

_____

_____

_____

_____

Name _____

Read. Then, answer the questions.

The Ink Monkey

Many years ago lived a man named Zhu Xi. He was a famous thinker. It was said that he had a tiny "ink monkey" for a pet. It sat on his desk. It handed him pens. It helped him make ink.

How could a monkey sleep in a paintbrush pot? That was so small! How could a monkey learn to make ink? That was so smart! It must have been a story! It had to be fiction!

In 2000, an American scientist discovered some bones in China. They were from a very old monkey. It was small, like a mouse. Some foot bones were as tiny as a grain of rice! The scientist, Dr. Dan Gebo, says that this monkey may be a missing link. A missing link is important. It can tell us more about how humans evolved. Gebo calls his discovery "the dawn monkey."

Is the dawn monkey related to the ink monkey? The dawn monkey is much smaller than we thought monkeys could be. So, we know that a tiny Chinese monkey did exist. Could this monkey be related to Zhu Xi's pet?

After Dr. Gebo's discovery came another surprise. The Chinese said that they had found a living ink monkey! It was found in a forest. Zhu Xi once lived near this very forest! But, the Chinese have not said anything more.

1. How does the author describe the foot bones of the monkey that the American scientist discovered?

   _____

2. Why does the author say the story of the ink monkey "had to be fiction?" Use details from the passage to explain your answer.

   _____

   _____

3. At the end of the passage, how does the discovery of the living monkey connect to the story of Zhu Xi?

   _____

   _____

✺ Reflect

Describe how the author connects the two monkeys discussed.

_____

_____

Read. Then, answer the questions.

Sweet Machines

Doughnuts have been sweet treats for centuries. The Dutch first made them as "oily cakes." Dutch cooks rolled small dough balls carefully by hand. Then the bakers dropped them one by one into a kettle of oil. But, the doughnuts did not cook all of the way through. So, the cooks filled the little cakes with raisins or jam.

Today, doughnut machines make thousands of them at one time. One machine stamps out doughnuts into round shapes. A moving belt carries them into a warming oven. Doughnuts contain yeast. Heat makes yeast puff up. The warming oven makes the doughnuts puff up. Then, the doughnuts plop into a big oil bath. This is not a water bath! The doughnuts fry in the hot oil. Once they are cooked, they land back on the belt.

Some doughnuts ride through a waterfall of sugar and milk glaze! This glaze coats the doughnuts.

Frosted doughnuts are dipped in flavored frosting before they finish their ride.

Some doughnuts have fillings such as cream or jam. At another machine, someone pushes each doughnut against a pipe. The pipe pumps delicious filling into the doughnut. Last stop: doughnut boxes!

1. Based on the passage, why did Dutch cooks fill the cakes with raisins or jam?

_____

2. What is the main purpose of the passage? Use details from the passage to explain your answer.

_____

_____

3. Based on paragraph five, how does the narrator feel about doughnuts that have fillings? Underline the details in the passage that explain your answer.

_____

✺ Reflect

Could the author have combined the third and fourth paragraphs into one? Why or why not? Use your understanding of main topics of paragraphs to explain your answer.

_____

_____

_____

_____

Name _____

Read. Then, answer the questions.

A Wild Ride

A roller coaster plunges down hills. It races around corners. It is exciting! And it is mostly run by nature!

A machine pulls the roller coaster cars up the first hill. On simple roller coasters, the machine is like a towrope. Chains help pull the cars up this hill, called the lift hill. Then, the chains are released. Gravity pulls the roller coaster down the hill. When it heads up another hill, gravity slows the roller coaster's tail end. That is why it slows down and speeds up during the ride.

Many roller coasters are built with hills that become smaller and smaller. The biggest hill is almost always the lift hill. This creates a lot of energy for the rest of the ride. As the roller coaster zooms over smaller hills, it starts to slow. Finally, it coasts to a stop.

Newer roller coasters are made of steel. Some run on tracks, like a train. Others run on rails, like a subway. Steel tracks are easier to bend. Steel roller coasters have more turns. Sometimes, the cars even flip upside down! The tracks are put together using very few joints. This makes the ride speedy and smooth. Two sets of wheels keep the cars from running off the tracks.

With thrilling twists, turns, and drops, it is no wonder that people love roller coasters!

1. What creates a lot of energy for a roller coaster ride? Underline the details in the passage that support your answer.

   _____

2. What makes the ride of the steel roller coasters speedy and smooth?

   _____

3. What is the main focus of the third paragraph? List supporting details from the passage.

   _____

   _____

☼ Reflect

Explain what the narrator means by a roller coaster is "mostly run by nature". Use details from the passage to explain your answer.

_____

_____

_____

Name _____

Read. Then, answer the questions.

Mozart's Life

Some people learn things slowly. Others are born with talent. Wolfgang Amadeus Mozart was born with talent. He made wonderful music. Mozart was a famous composer. He was even famous as a child!

At three years old, Mozart played the piano. He played real songs! At five years old, he wrote his own music. Mozart played all over Europe. Sometimes, his father blindfolded young Mozart. Then, his father held him above the piano. Mozart was hanging upside down! He could not see the piano keys. But, he still played perfectly! Mozart amazed everyone who heard him.

At seven years old, Mozart started to publish his music. Now, other people could buy it. By age eight, he had taught himself to play the organ and violin. He also wrote longer music. At age 13, Mozart wrote his first **opera**. An opera is a musical work. It is like a play. But, the parts are not spoken. They are sung.

Mozart traveled a lot. He was not at home much. He was not really happy. Few people were as smart as he was. But, in other ways, Mozart was not smart. When he grew up, he spent too much money. He found it hard to make enough money. Mozart died young. He was only 35 years old. But, his music is still alive. It is played and loved all over the world.

1. When did Mozart start to publish his own music?

_____

2. Based on the passage, what is an *opera*?

_____

3. How did Mozart amaze everyone who heard him? Use details from the passage to explain your answer.

_____

_____

☀ Reflect

In the fourth paragraph, the author tells us that Mozart was not really happy. How do you think Mozart could have been happier? Use details from the passage to support your thinking.

_____

_____

Read. Then, answer the questions.

The Businessman

When Cameron Johnson was seven years old, his mother gave him some tomatoes. He wanted to sell them. A woman asked him how much they were. He asked for one dollar each. The woman said that was too much. But, Cameron did not change his price. He knew that someone else might pay a dollar.

Cameron knows how to sell things. When he was nine years old, he got his first computer. Did he play computer games? No. He started his first business! He made special cards on his computer. Then, he sold them. He started selling things online. He sold his sister's stuffed animals. He bought more stuffed animals. He sold them too. He was selling 40 animals each day! Cameron made $50,000 that year. He was 12 years old.

How did Cameron learn how to do this? His family helped. His great-grandfather started as a car dealer. His father runs the company today. Cameron's parents talked to him about money. He learned how to save his money. He learned how to keep track of it too. Cameron has great ideas. He **acts** instead of just talking about things.

Cameron says that you do not have to make a lot of money to be happy. Businesses can be big or small. No one is too old or too young to give business a try.

1. How did Cameron learn about money and starting his own business?

_____

_____

2. What is the main topic of the second paragraph?

_____

_____

3. Based on the passage, what does *act* mean? Underline the details in the passage that tell the reader how Cameron *acts*.

_____

Reflect

How was Cameron different from other children his age? Use details from the passage to explain your answer.

_____

_____

_____

_____

Name _____

Read. Then, answer the questions.

On the Ice

A girl skated onto the ice. The crowd was silent. Her skating was powerful. She moved with the music. She glided with feeling. Sixteen-year-old Kristi Yamaguchi won two awards that day. **No one was surprised**.

The next year, Kristi skated at the World Junior Championships. She won the gold medal! Kristi kept pushing herself. In four more years, she won 14 other first-place medals. Then, she skated at the 1992 Winter Olympics.

Kristi was born with clubbed feet. She wore casts on her legs. Later, she wore special shoes. She had trouble walking. Her legs were weak. Kristi's mother wanted her to dance. This would strengthen Kristi's legs. But, when Kristi was four years old, she watched the Olympic Games on TV. She told her mother that she wanted to skate.

Kristi practiced a lot, six days a week. She got up at four o'clock in the morning. She skated for five hours. After school, she went to skating lessons. Kristi did this for 10 years!

At the Olympics, Kristi had fun. And, it showed! Kristi said later that there are not many times when a skater knows that she skated perfectly. For her, the Olympics was one of those times. She won the gold medal. And, she proved that hard work pays off.

1. What did the author mean by stating that "No one was surprised"?

_____

_____

2. What is the main topic of the passage? What is the main topic of the fourth paragraph?

_____

_____

3. How are the main topic of the passage and the fourth paragraph related?

_____

_____

☀ Reflect

Describe the connection the author makes between Kristi's hard work and her successes. Use details from the passage to explain your answer.

_____

_____

Name _____

Read. Then, answer the questions.

A Brave Conductor

It took courage for slaves to try to escape from the South. In 1849, Harriet Tubman escaped. She used the Underground Railroad and followed the North Star. She started in Dorchester County, Maryland. She ended in Philadelphia, Pennsylvania. Slaves were free in the North. She knew she could live there as a free person.

Then, Harriet did something very brave. Harriet went back to the South! She worked as a conductor on the Underground Railroad. She helped other slaves escape. It was a dangerous job. Harriet helped about 300 slaves reach freedom in the North.

In 1861, the American Civil War began. Harriet became a spy for the North. She knew the land. She had traveled through it many times in the dark. Harriet could pose as a slave. She learned information to help the army in the North.

When African Americans could become soldiers, Harriet helped them too. Harriet and the soldiers freed more than 700 slaves during a bold raid.

Harriet was also a nurse. She took care of injured soldiers and slaves. When the war was over, Harriet still worked. She fought for the rights of women and freed slaves. She opened a home in Auburn, New York, where she cared for aging African Americans. Harriet died there in 1913.

1. Why did Harriet Tubman want to escape to the North?

_____

2. What did Harriet do that was very brave? Underline the details in the passage that support your answer.

_____

_____

3. Describe the connection the passage makes between Harriet Tubman and the American Civil War.

_____

_____

☀ Reflect

Based on the passage, how would you describe Harriet Tubman's personality? Use details from the passage to explain your answer.

_____

_____

Name _____

Read. Then, answer the questions.

Guiding Star

Sacagawea knew about life in strange places. Her tribe, the Shoshone, was raided. Sacagawea was taken captive. Her home was now with the enemy.

Four years later, Sacagawea married a French trader. That winter, a group of white men arrived. They camped near the village. The leaders were Meriwether Lewis and William Clark. President Thomas Jefferson had hired them to explore west of the Missouri River. Lewis and Clark needed to travel from the Missouri River to the Pacific Ocean.

Lewis and Clark heard of Sacagawea. They were headed west toward the Shoshone land. Sacagawea had been born there. She knew the country. Sacagawea could help them trade for horses they needed to cross the mountains. They hired her and her husband.

Sacagawea was an American Indian woman. Other Indians saw her with the white men. This made them trust the explorers. Sacagawea interpreted their words. She helped the white men talk to different tribes. Sacagawea guided them west.

Lewis and Clark came to a Shoshone village. They needed to trade for horses. This village was the home of Sacagawea's brother! Sacagawea still chose to travel all of the way to the Pacific Ocean with Lewis and Clark.

1. What were Lewis and Clark hired to do by President Jefferson?

   _____

2. What is the main topic of the first paragraph?

   _____

3. Why did Lewis and Clark need Sacagawea on their journey? Use details from the passage to explain your answer.

   _____

   _____

Reflect

Describe the connection between the title of the passage and the history of Sacagawea detailed in the passage.

   _____

   _____

   _____

Read. Then, answer the questions.

End of the Darkness

In 1882, baby Helen became very sick. When she got better, something was still wrong. She could not see. She could not hear. Helen Keller was blind and deaf.

Helen was like a wild animal. She screamed. She broke dishes. She threw chairs. Her parents wanted to help her. They met with Alexander Graham Bell, who worked with deaf children. He found a teacher for Helen named Anne Sullivan. Anne was almost fully blind herself.

Anne helped Helen calm down. She learned to sit at a table. She ate neatly. She stopped throwing things. Anne tried to teach Helen how to spell words with her fingers. She would give Helen something, such as a doll. Then, she would spell the word in Helen's hand. But, Helen did not understand.

In 1887, Anne finally broke through to Helen's **lonely** world. The teacher pumped water into Helen's hands. Then, she spelled the word water. Suddenly, Helen understood that Anne's movements were words. The words told her about the world. Helen learned 30 words that very day!

Anne stayed with Helen for the rest of her life. They toured the world together. In 1903, Helen wrote *The Story of My Life* (CreateSpace Independent Publishing Platform, 2014). Helen received many awards. She was given the Presidential Medal of Freedom. Helen Keller and Anne Sullivan's story still gives hope to blind and deaf people today.

1. What caused Helen Keller to become blind and deaf?

_____

2. How was Helen finally able to understand words? Underline the details in the passage that support your answer.

_____

_____

3. Why does the author describe Helen's world as *lonely*?

_____

✺ Reflect

Would Helen Keller have become so accomplished if she did not have her teacher, Anne Sullivan? Why or why not? Use details from the passage to explain your answer.

_____

_____

_____

Name _____

Read. Then, answer the questions.

As Dry as a Bone

The Atacama Desert is in Chile. It has not rained in parts of the desert for 400 years! The desert gets less than one-third of an inch (0.85 cm) of water every year. Most of this comes from fog. The Atacama is one of the driest places on Earth.

The Amazon River is on one side of the desert. The Pacific Ocean is on the other side. The Andes Mountains are in the way and hold the rain over the Amazon rain forest. The rain cannot reach the desert.

The Atacama is not a hot desert. It is cool. That is because it is high. The average height above sea level is almost 8,000 feet (2,438.4 m). Temperatures range from 32°F (0°C) to 77°F (25°C).

The Atacama is a harsh place. But, plants and animals always find a way to survive. Plants must have long roots to reach water deep in the ground. Insects and some animals, such as foxes and llamas, eat the plants.

People also live there. They live in tiny villages across the desert. They live in large towns along the ocean coast. Tourists visit these towns. And, sometimes they visit the Atacama Desert too.

1. What is the main topic of the passage?

_____

2. Describe some of the life that is found in the Atacama Desert and how it survives. Use details from the passage to explain your answer.

_____

_____

_____

3. How is the Atacama Desert different from what most people think of a typical desert? Underline the details in the passage that support your answer.

_____

_____

☀ Reflect

What makes the Atacama Desert such a harsh place? Use details from the passage to explain your answer.

_____

_____

_____

Name _____

Read. Then, answer the questions.

The Amazing Amazon

Water runs from rivers into seas. River water is fresh. Seawater is salty. About one-fifth of the freshwater on Earth comes from one river called the Amazon River. This river is in South America, near the Amazon rain forest.

The Amazon River starts high in the Andes Mountains. It is more than 4,000 miles (6,437.38 km) long. Water flows from the Amazon River into the Atlantic Ocean. A river mouth is where a river meets the sea. River water dumps into the sea. The Amazon River carries a lot of water. Its mouth has to be huge. The Amazon river mouth is 150 miles (241.4 km) wide!

Explorers discovered the river mouth in 1500, while sailing on the Atlantic Ocean. They were 200 miles (321.87 km) from land. But, they were not sailing on saltwater. They were sailing on freshwater from the mouth of the Amazon River!

The Amazon River has not changed much since then. People cut down a lot of rain forest trees. Few people live there. There are no bridges built across the Amazon. Maybe that is why the Amazon has so many strange creatures.

1. What is the difference between river water and seawater?

_____

2. How did early explorers discover the mouth of the Amazon River in 1500?

_____

3. What reasons does the author give for why so many strange creatures live in the Amazon River?

_____

_____

☀ Reflect

How does the author seem to feel about the Amazon River and its importance in the world? Use details from the passage to explain your answer.

_____

_____

_____

_____

_____

_____

Name _____

Read. Then, answer the questions.

Changing with the Seasons

People are not the only ones to change the way we dress with the seasons. We change our clothing with the seasons to protect us from the weather. Animals do the same to protect themselves when the seasons change. They know when it is time to change.

For example, the arctic fox has a thick, white fur coat in the winter. A white coat is not easy to see in the snow. This helps the fox hide from enemies. When spring comes, the fox's fur changes to brown. It is then the color of the ground.

The ptarmigan, or snow chicken, has white feathers in the winter. It too is hard to see in the snow. In the spring, the bird molts. This means that it sheds all of its feathers. The bird grows new feathers that are speckled. When the bird is very still, it looks like a rock.

1. How does the author compare people and the arctic fox in the passage?

   _____

   _____

2. Describe something that the arctic fox and the snow chicken have in common.

   _____

   _____

3. What is the author's main purpose for writing the passage?

   _____

   _____

   _____

Reflect

Describe how the image supports the author's purpose for writing the passage.

_____

_____

_____

Name _____

Read. Then, answer the questions.

The Birds in My Garden

I like to watch the birds in my garden. The robins came as the snow was melting. The male robin has a red chest. He helped his mate build a nest in the cherry tree. I peeked into the nest. I counted three tiny eggs.

Two magpies live in my garden. Their feathers are shiny black and white. The magpies built their huge nest in the pine tree. Magpies can copy the sounds of other birds. They are noisy.

My favorite birds to watch are quail. They have topknots on their heads that bob when they walk. Quail make their nests on the ground under bushes. They live in groups called **flocks**. They can run very fast. When they are frightened, they scatter to different places. When the danger is gone, they whistle to each other to come back. I love watching the baby quail follow their parents.

1. In what season did the robins come to the author's garden? How do you know?

_____

2. Based on the passage, what are *flocks*? Which kind of bird described in the passage lives in a *flock*?

_____

_____

3. What is the author's main purpose for writing this passage?

_____

_____

Reflect

In the passage, the author describes where the birds build their nests. Describe the differences between the three birds and their nests. Use details from the passage to explain your answer.

_____

_____

_____

Name _____

Read. Then, answer the questions.

The Ladybug

The ladybug is a very interesting insect. It is also called a ladybird beetle. Most ladybugs are red or yellow with black spots. The California ladybug's shell is yellow with black spots. The ladybug has a tiny head and no neck. Its body is round and shaped like half a pea. It can run very fast on its short legs. The ladybug's wings are tucked under its shell. It can fly very well.

The ladybug lays its eggs on the underside of green leaves. When the grubs hatch, they are very hungry. They quickly start to eat plant lice. Lice are insects that hurt plants. They can ruin a farmer's crop. Fruit growers like ladybugs because they eat harmful lice.

The California ladybug was brought to the United States from Australia. It helps protect orange, lemon, and grapefruit trees.

1. Where does a ladybug with a yellow shell and black spots most likely live?

   _____

2. What are ladybugs called when they first hatch?

   _____

3. What is the main topic of the first paragraph?

   _____

   _____

4. Would an apple orchard farmer benefit from having ladybugs? Why or why not? Use details from the passage to explain your answer.

   _____

   _____

☀ Reflect

Was it helpful to bring ladybugs from Australia to California? Use details from the passage to explain your answer.

_____

_____

_____

Name _____

Read. Then, answer the questions.

Ants

Ants can be found almost anywhere on our planet. Earth has about 12,000 different types of ants. Ants are amazing insects. An ant can carry things many times its weight. Ants use feelers on top of their heads to find food.

Many ants have very sharp teeth. An ant's jaw opens sideways. Ants use their jaws to eat. They also use their jaws to carry their babies and to fight. Ants are social insects. They live in large groups called **colonies**.

1. Based on the passage, where can someone find ants?

   _____

2. How do ants find food?

   _____

3. Based on the passage, what are *colonies*? Underline the details in the passage that support your answer.

   _____

4. What is the main purpose of the passage? How do you know?

   _____

   _____

☀ Reflect

After reading the passage, what do you think are some other details that the author could have included to teach us more about ants?

_____

_____

Name _____

Read. Then, answer the questions.

The Koala

Koalas live in Australia. They spend most of their time high up in tall eucalyptus trees. Koalas eat the leaves from the tree. They eat about two to three pounds of leaves every day. They drink very little water. The eucalyptus leaves give koalas the water they need.

Many people think koalas are bears because they look like bear cubs. Koalas are not bears. They are marsupials. Marsupials are special kinds of mammal. They have pouches to keep their babies warm and safe. Koalas have pouches just like another animal that begins with a *k*. Can you guess what it is? It is a kangaroo.

1. Why do koalas not drink a lot of water? Use details from the passage to explain your answer.

_____

_____

2. What is the difference between a koala and a bear?

_____

_____

3. Why did the author need to describe the difference between a koala and a bear?

_____

_____

4. What is the main purpose of the passage? How do you know?

_____

_____

☀ Reflect

If you wanted to research other animals similar to koalas and kangaroos, what word in the passage could help you do your research? Why is this word helpful?

_____

_____

Read. Then, answer the questions.

Germs

Germs are things you should not share. Germs can make you sick. Even though you cannot see germs, they get into a body in many ways. Germs get in the body through the nose, mouth, eyes, and cuts in the skin. We share germs when we sneeze or cough and do not cover our mouths. We share germs when we drink from the same cup or eat from the same plate.

To keep germs to yourself and to stay well:

- Wash your hands with soap.
- Cover your mouth when you cough or sneeze.
- Do not share food or drink.
- Keep your fingers out of your nose, mouth, and eyes.
- Drink a lot of water.
- Get a lot of fresh air.
- Eat healthful meals.
- Get plenty of sleep.

1. Why should you not share germs?

_____

2. Where can germs enter the body?

_____

3. What is the main purpose of the passage? How do you know?

_____

_____

Reflect

Why did the author include the bulleted list in the passage? What does it add to the passage?

_____

_____

_____

_____

Name _____

Read. Then, answer the questions.

Trees

Trees can be placed into two groups: evergreen and deciduous. Evergreen trees stay green throughout the cold winter. Their leaves are often like needles. Christmas trees are evergreens.

Deciduous trees lose their leaves in autumn and grow new ones in the spring. They may have flowers or fruit that grow on them. The trees that turn red, orange, and yellow in autumn are deciduous.

1. What is the main topic of the passage?

_____

2. What is the main topic of the first paragraph?

_____

_____

3. Based on the passage, what are *deciduous* trees?

_____

_____

4. How are the leaves on evergreens and deciduous trees different?

_____

_____

Reflect

Why are evergreens used most often as Christmas trees? Use details from the passage to explain your answer.

_____

_____

_____

_____

_____

Name _____

Read. Then, answer the questions.

A Tasty Butterfly

Butterflies are lovely to look at, but here is how to make one you can eat!

Ingredients:

    2 frozen pancakes
    1 banana
    jelly or jam
    2 grapes
    2 pieces of link sausage
    2 toothpicks

Directions:

• Toast the pancakes and cut them in half. This will make four pieces because a butterfly has four wings.

• Peel the banana and place it on a plate. This will be the butterfly's body.

• Spread jelly or jam on the "wings."

• Use the toothpicks to hold the grapes on the banana as eyes.

• With an adult, cook the sausages and place them at the top of the banana as antennae.

1. What are the toothpicks used for?

_____

2. In the third step, why has the author put the word *wings* in quotation marks?

_____

_____

3. Why does the author tell the reader to cut the two pancakes in half?

_____

_____

☀ Reflect

The author lists the directions but does not number them. Do you think the directions need to be completed in a certain order? Use details from the passage to explain your answer.

_____

Name _____

Read. Then, answer the questions.

A Sunny Flower

A sunflower starts as a seed and begins to grow a strong taproot. Soon, the green **stalk** begins to grow toward the warmth of the sun. As the plant grows, it forms a bud that will someday become a flower. The plant faces east as the sun rises in the morning. Then, it follows the sun across the sky until it is facing west when the sun sets. As the flower's bud blooms, it unfolds into large golden petals. The center of the flower is full of seeds. The seeds can be eaten or planted so that more sunny flowers can grow!

1. Based on the passage, what is a *stalk*?

_____

2. Where do the seeds of a sunflower grow?

_____

3. Why does a sunflower face west in the afternoon?

_____

_____

☀ Reflect

What is the author explaining to the reader in the passage? Use details from the passage to explain your answer.

_____

_____

_____

_____

_____

_____

_____

_____

Read. Then, answer the questions.

Hurricanes

Hurricanes are huge storms that begin at sea. Warm air from the ocean rises toward the sky. Then, cool air begins swirling around the warm air. As water from the ocean is lifted into the air, a storm begins to form. Soon, huge thunderclouds begin to drop rain in heavy sheets. The storm spins like a top across the water and may even reach land. The hurricane will not die until it passes over cooler water or crosses land.

Hurricanes have different names in other parts of the world. They are called **cyclones** in the Indian Ocean. When this type of storm forms in the western Pacific Ocean, it is called a typhoon. In the Atlantic Ocean and the eastern North Pacific Ocean, they are called hurricanes. No matter what the name, they are huge, spinning storms.

1. How is a hurricane formed?

_____

_____

_____

2. When does a hurricane die?

_____

_____

3. Based on the passage, what is a *cyclone*? How are hurricanes and cyclones related?

_____

4. What is the main focus of the second paragraph?

_____

_____

_____

☀ Reflect

Why does the author call hurricanes "huge, spinning storms" at the end of the passage? Use details from the passage to explain your answer.

_____

_____

_____

Name _____

Read. Then, answer the questions.

Barn Owls

Barn owls can be found all over the world. They live in grasslands, open woodlands, and farmlands where they can easily find food. Barn owls swoop over fields, listening for mice and rats. They can hear them from a quarter of a mile away! When a barn owl finds one, it drops down and catches the mouse or rat with its sharp claws. A family of barn owls can eat more than 20,000 mice and rats in a year!

A mother and father barn owl stay together for life. They make their homes in old barns and hollow trees, but they do not build nests as other birds do. The mother owl lays five to nine eggs, and they hatch about one month later.

In some places, barn owls are dying. People put poison out to chase mice away, but then the barn owls eat the sick mice. Barn owls are also having trouble finding places to lay eggs because many old trees are cut down. We should all work together to help save the barn owls.

1. What reason does the author give for barn owls living in grasslands, open woodlands, and farmlands?

   _____

2. How are barn owls different from other birds? Use details from the passage to explain your answer.

   _____

3. What is the main topic of the third paragraph? What details tell you this?

   _____

   _____

Reflect

What are some things that people can do to help stop barn owls from dying? Use details from the passage to explain your answer.

_____

_____

_____

_____

_____

_____

Name _____

Read. Then, answer the questions.

Get Out of My House

Millions of termites work together to build large dirt mounds in the grassy plains of Africa, Australia, and South America. After their work is done, many other animals come along to use the mounds, each in their own way.

Because the mounds are often the highest part of the land, some animals use them to get a better view. A mother cheetah and her babies may climb a mound and stand on top to look for food. The mother then leaves her babies on the mound to watch her hunt. This is how they learn to hunt for themselves.

Other animals use the mounds to find food. Aardvarks use their sharp claws to dig through the walls of the mounds. Then, they stick their long noses through the holes to make a meal of termites.

With a hole through it, a termite mound becomes the perfect home for a mongoose family. They live in groups of 12 to 15 members and work together to watch for enemies. The termite mound makes a great lookout!

Some animals use the mounds for something quite funny—to scratch themselves. Elephants and rhinos get itchy skin from bug bites, scratches, and dry mud. They stand near the mounds and rub themselves on them. Sometimes they stand over the mounds to scratch their bellies!

Who would ever think a small bug like a termite could be so important to so many other animals?

1. Based on the passage, how do termite mounds help baby cheetahs learn to hunt for themselves?

_____

2. What is the main topic of the third paragraph?

_____

3. What reason does the author give for why elephants and rhinos use the termite mounds?

_____

_____

☀ Reflect

From all of the animals described, which animal might the termites not want using their termite mounds? Why? Use details from the passage to explain your answer.

_____

_____

Name _____

Read. Then, answer the questions.

Gorillas

Gorillas live in the mountains and forests of Zaire, which is in Africa. Because they are peaceful animals, scientists have been lucky enough to study them. They have found that gorillas live in groups made up of several females, their babies, and one or more males. Baby gorillas do not live with their mothers long enough. After only three years, they set off on their own. Each evening, gorillas build nests to sleep in by picking leaves and laying on them. Gorillas eat tasty foods that include fruits, leaves, and juicy stems. Gorillas are becoming **extinct** because their forests are being destroyed. We should help save their forests and mountains.

1. How long do baby gorillas live with their mothers?

_____

2. What do you think is the author's main purpose for writing the passage?

_____

_____

3. Based on the passage, what does *extinct* mean?

_____

☀ Reflect

Why do you think the author ends the passage by telling readers they should help save the gorillas' forests and mountains?

_____

_____

_____

_____

_____

Name _____

Read. Then, answer the questions.

Bird Beaks

Even though they have wings and lay eggs, birds are not all the same. By looking closely at birds' beaks, you can learn a lot about them

- A large, sharp, curved beak tells you that the bird is a meat eater. The hooked shape of the beak helps the bird tear skin from its prey before eating it.

- Birds with straight, sharp beaks often feed on insects and worms. They will also dig into the ground to look for worms or caterpillars.

- Birds with short, curved beaks are seed-eating birds. The short beaks are strong enough to crack through the tough outer shells of seeds and nuts.

- A few birds have long, thin beaks that they use to suck nectar from flowers.

1. Based on the passage, how are birds alike?

   _____

2. What is one way that you can learn a lot about a bird?

   _____

3. Where would you most likely find a bird with a straight, sharp beak looking for food? Use details from the passage to explain your answer.

   _____

 **Reflect**

Why do you think the author used bullets in the passage? Use details from the passage to explain your answer.

_____

_____

_____

_____

_____

Answer Key

Answers will vary but may include the answers provided. Accept all reasonable answers as long as students have proper evidence and support.

Page 5
1. by bus; 2. how she misses her family; She slumps down as she says it, which shows that she is sad or upset. 3. She gives her a snack and then plays a card game with her.

Page 6
1. the hospital; 2. by looking at the X-ray; 3. a questionable situation that may cause harm; For Brandon, it is a situation where he might hurt his arm even more.

Page 7
1. a storm; 2. *pitter-patter, pitter-pat, tapping*; 3. The last words of the lines in each stanza rhyme.

Page 8
1. riding his bike, starting swimming lessons, or visiting his grandparents; 2. excited; "I had a blast last year when we went there." 3. Nick plans to catch a fish bigger than the pans they have cooked fish in before. 4. It is time for Nick to finish the letter and go.

Page 9
1. when exploring; 2. how to get the large cookies back to their families; 3. The first ant takes the cookie in small pieces, and the second ant wants to take the whole cookie at once.

Page 10
1. to go hungry because of lack of food; 2. He goes out to find more food. 3. He always worries that he will not have enough food and that something will happen to the food he has.

Page 11
1. The king is taking some of their food and storing it away in the castle. 2. careful about spending money or using things when you do not need them; 3. At first, they were mad at the king for taking some of their food away and leaving them hungry. In the end, they are glad he stored food because it helped feed them during the famine.

Page 12
1. the tree; 2. they are both green and are both Mother Nature's gifts; 3. happy; At the end of the poem, the author says they both make him sing.

Page 13
1. ladders; 2. the tools and uniforms firefighters use; 3. to put out a fire

Page 14
1. He did not have a paintbrush to use. 2. to get something; 3. Ma Lien is a caring person because he uses his special paintbrush to help people. 3. He responds by doing what the king asks but makes it so that the king cannot have what he wants.

Page 15
1. He holds a piece of wood over his head. 2. No, because the text uses the word *suddenly* to describe how the rain starts. 3. Fireball opens his mother's hand to see what she is holding.

Page 16
1. He is too old for a teddy bear and Ted is getting worn. 2. Ted is worn. He is missing patches of fur, missing an eye, and has been sewn a few times. 3. The last words of the lines in each stanza rhyme.

Page 17
1. upset; She shouts at him, calls him foolish, and says, "I wish you would think!" 2. makes sense or is right

Page 18
1. She sees her reflection in the river. 2. They agree saying , "Yes, you are big," and then go away. 3. She feels small, but she does not mind it.

Page 19
1. gold; 2. soldiers; 3. They both consist of stanzas where the last word in each line rhymes.

Page 20
1. a person who cuts down trees; 2. They are both very big. Check students' underlining. 3. He helps by carrying the wood that Paul cuts down and by carrying water to the loggers using a tub on his back.

Page 21
1. the grasslands; Check students' underlining. 2. He helps him find his home. 3. He thinks they will all beg to have him back.

Page 22
1. gigantic; 2. It is broken into smaller and smaller pieces and shared with the author's friends. 3. She makes a joke.

Page 23
1. as a peaceful place; Check students' examples. 2. from peaceful to stormy; huge waves start crashing on the shore, the clouds darken, and the wind picks up; 3. likes, admires, loves

Page 24
1. to display it at the American Indian fair; 2. He does not really care about what he is making or how it iss going to look. 3. She cares about the project and how it is going to look.

Page 25
1. the grasslands; Check students' underlining. 2. The giraffes ran for cover and hid behind the thickest and tallest trees. 3. No, because the falcon is a small animal and will not have as large or destructive a sneeze as an elephant.

Page 26
1. He wants help because his house is too noisy. 2. bring his dog, his cow, and his horse inside to live with him; 3. Without all of the animals, his house seems quieter in comparison.

Page 27
1. not satisfied; She disagrees with Father Rat and suggests something different. 2. It was more powerful than the cloud. 3. The wall shows Mother and Father Rat that he is not powerful because he cannot stop the noble rat from passing through the holes in him. The Daughter Rat marries the noble rat, and they live happily ever after.

Page 28
1. how toucans live together; 2. The toucan's feet have two pairs of toes that face opposite ways. Their tongues are hairy. 3. Although the tongue may look like a feather, it is not soft like a feather.

Page 29
1. to save energy; 2. Other animals typically live far away from people, but sloths do not seem afraid of people, and will live near villages. 3. Sloths live in trees and eat leaves, so they live where they get food.

Page 30
1. Dolphins breathe air. 2. how dolphins use body language to communicate; 3. They make many different sounds and use body language.

Page 31
1. in the Lincoln Bedroom; 2. strange; 3. They are all famous.

Page 32
1. as tiny as a grain of rice; 2. A monkey would not be small enough to fit in a paintbrush pot or smart enough to learn to make ink. 3. The monkey was found in a forest near where Zhu Xi lived.

Page 33

1. They did not cook the cakes all the way through. 2. to explain how doughnuts are made; 3. They are delicious. Check students' underlining.

Page 34

1. the lift hill and gravity; Check students' underlining. 2. The tracks are put together with very few joints. 3. the hills in a roller coaster

Page 35

1. at seven years old; 2. a musical work like a play where the parts are not spoken but sung; 3. He could play the piano perfectly while blindfolded and while hanging upside down.

Page 36

1. His parents and his grandfather set good examples and taught him how to deal with money. 2. how well Cameron sold things; 3. to do something; Check students' underlining.

Page 37

1. Kristi skated so well that day that everyone thought she deserved to win the awards. 2. the life and accomplishments of the famous ice skater Kristi Yamaguchi; how she prepared for the Olympics; 3. Her preparation is one of the reasons for her successes throughout her life.

Page 38

1. Slaves were free in the North, and she could live as a free person there. 2. She returned to the South and helped other slaves escape to the North. Check students' underlining. 3. Harriet was a spy for the North. She pretended to be a slave and helped by giving information to the army in the North.

Page 39

1. explore the western part of North America; 2. to describe how Sacagawea was taken from her tribe; 3. They needed Sacagawea because she knew the land and could guide them, she could help them trade for horses, she could help them gain the trust of the Indians, and she could interpret for them.

Page 40

1. an illness when she was a baby; 2. Anne Sullivan pumped water into Helen's hands, and then spelled the word *water* in her hands. Check students' underlining. 3. because she could not communicate with others.

Page 41

1. the Atacama Desert in Chile; 2. Plants with long roots can reach the water sources deep in the ground. Insects, foxes, and llamas survive by eating the plants. 3. It is not hot. Check students' underlining.

Page 42

1. River water is freshwater; seawater is saltwater. 2. Early explorers realized they were not sailing on saltwater, even though they were 200 miles from land. 3. Few people live there, and no bridges are built across the river.

Page 43

1. Both people and arctic foxes change the way they dress for the seasons. 2. They both change to white in the winter because it is a hard color to see in the snow. 3. to describe how two animals change when the seasons change

Page 44

1. spring; The author states that they come as the snow is melting. 2. groups of birds that live together; quail; 3. to describe the birds in the author's garden

Page 45

1. California or Australia; 2. grubs; 3. ladybugs' features; 4. Yes. Ladybugs eat harmful lice that could damage apple trees.

Page 46

1. almost anywhere on our planet; 2. They use the feelers on the tops of their heads. 3. large groups that ants live in; Check students' underlining. 4. to teach the reader about ants; The author tells the reader many different facts about ants in the passage.

Page 47

1. The eucalyptus leaves they eat give them the water they need. 2. A koala has a pouch on her body to keep her babies warm and safe. A bear does not have a pouch. 3. Many people think that koalas are bears. 4. to teach the reader about koalas; The author tells the reader information about koalas.

Page 48

1. They can make people sick. 2. through the nose, mouth, eyes, and cuts in the skin; 3. to teach about germs and give suggestions about how to avoid germs to stay healthy

Page 49

1. someone who collects stamps; 2. tweezers and an album with plastic pages; 3. how to collect and organize stamps

Page 50

1. special kinds of paper, stickers, cutouts, letters, scissors, and albums; 2. the difference between scrapbooks and photo albums; 3. Scrapbooks include writing and mementos, not just pictures.

Page 51

1. *There's a Nightmare in my Closet, Just for You,* or *A Boy, a Dog, and a Frog;* 2. His father was in the US Navy so they moved around a lot. 3. The first paragraph focuses on his writing and the second paragraph focuses on his personal life. Both support the main topic of the life of Mercer Mayer.

Page 52

1. for her mother's birthday; 2. She may tear the cake. 3. to explain the steps to frosting a cake so that Jessica can do it on her own

Page 53

1. Chemicals are everywhere. Check students' underling. 2. in the air, homes, food, and our bodies; 3. when chemicals mix to form something new; a banana ripening or baking cupcakes

Page 54

1. the youngest player; 2. to explain how to play The Great Race; 3. It gives instructions on what to do if you land on a certain space and what direction players should move.

Page 55

1. the two main types of trees; 2. evergreen trees; 3. trees that lose their leaves in autumn and grow new ones in the spring; 4. The leaves on evergreens are like needles and stay green. The leaves on deciduous trees are many shapes and change color and fall off each year.

Page 56

1. to hold the grapes on the bananas; 2. The wings are not truly wings, but pancakes. 3. to make four pieces, because a butterfly has four wings

Page 57

1. a plant's stem; 2. in the center of the flower; 3. That is where the sun is at that time of day.

Page 58

1. Warm air from the ocean rises toward the sky, cool air swirls around the warm air, and the water that is lifted forms a storm. 2. when it passes over cooler water or crosses land; 3. a hurricane in the Indian Ocean; They are related because they are the same type of storm, but are formed in different locations on Earth. 4. Hurricanes have different names depending on where they form.

Page 59

1. Those are the places where they can easily find food. 2. They do not build nests. 3. why barn owls are dying; Barn owls eat mice that people have poisoned. People also cut down the trees barn owls live in.

Page 60

1. Termite mounds give baby cheetahs a place to sit up high and watch their mothers hunt. 2. how aardvarks use the termite mounds to find food; 3. Elephants and rhinos use the termite mounds to scratch their bodies when they are itchy.

Page 61

1. three years; 2. to teach the reader about gorillas; 3. no longer existing

Page 62

1. All birds have wings and lay eggs. 2. looking closely at the bird's beak; 3. on the ground; They dig into the ground to look for worms or caterpillars.